mix & match
QUILTS
With the **AccuQuilt GO!**®

Edited by Elisa Sims Albury

HOUSE of
WHITE
BIRCHES

PUBLISHERS
SINCE 1947

Table of Contents

Introduction

All quilters are familiar with the classic shapes used in traditional quiltmaking. Combinations of squares, rectangles, triangles and parallelograms are the workhorses of the quilting world. Four- and Nine-Patch blocks, half- and quarter-square triangles, and flying geese serve as the basis for many traditional quilts. When combined, these pieces form an almost endless number of traditional block designs.

These design elements have stayed the same as the tools we use to make them have changed over time. Enter the AccuQuilt GO!® fabric-cutting system and the Mix & Match die set. This new tool takes cutting quilt pieces to a whole new level. With it, you can cut more layers of fabric, of the exact same shape, in less time.

We've put the GO!® cutter into the hands of some of our favorite designers to create 12 fresh quilts from traditional to contemporary styles all based upon the simple shapes contained in the Mix & Match die set. We've got you covered from bed quilts for kids and adults to a fun quilt for toddlers, plus unique quilted items for tabletops. Come along as we "mix" things up a bit. Less time cutting means more time for quilting. Let's get GO-ing!

General Instructions

These general instructions are intended as guidelines for the cutting and construction techniques used in all of the quilt patterns in this book. Each project in *Mix & Match Quilts With the AccuQuilt GO!®* is made with a selection of shapes from the Mix & Match die set. Refer to these general instructions or the materials that came with your cutter for guidance on using your machine.

The AccuQuilt® die shapes used in this book include the GO! Mix & Match die set (A–H), the 2½" strip cutter (55017), GO! Circle set (55012) and GO! Funky Flowers (55042). Don't worry if you do not own the strip cutter die. Instead, cut the number of 2½" strips needed with a rotary cutter and cutting mat. Additionally, templates for the circle and flower appliqué shapes are included for your use in this book.

For your convenience we've also included a handy die guide at the top of the first page of each project.

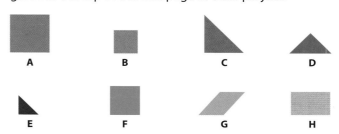

This guide illustrates the dies, A–H, that are used in each particular pattern. The dies that are used in the pattern appear in color, so that, at a glance, you can see which shapes to use.

Let's get started!

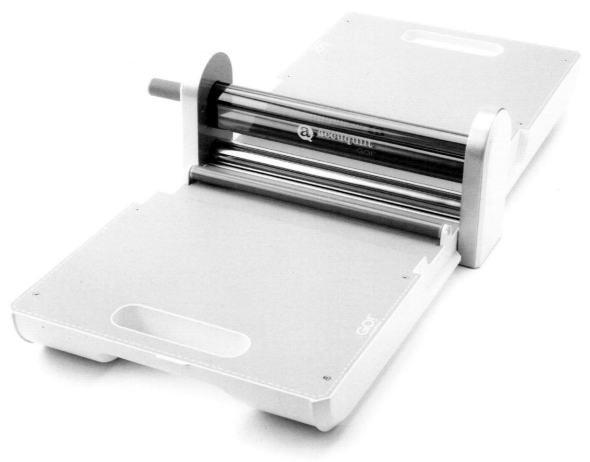

Using Your AccuQuilt GO! Cutter

To use the AccuQuilt GO!® Fabric Cutter, first precut appropriately sized strips to feed through the cutter. These strips can be layered or fan-folded to cut multiple shapes in one pass. The Fabric Reference Chart on page 5 shows precut strip sizes, fan-fold widths, number of shapes (cuts) that can be made from one fabric-strip length and the approximate number of shapes that can be made from a single yard of fabric for the die shapes used in this book. All fabric yardages have been calculated assuming a 40" usable width.

The GO! cutter can cut up to six layers of cotton quilting fabric at a time. However, it is suggested that you begin with fewer fabric layers and build up with increased skill and experience so as to avoid jamming the machine. Even the same type of fabric is not always the same thickness. The properties of quilting cotton can vary from brand to brand. For best results, use the cutter on a flat, hard, clean surface so the rubber feet can grip and hold the cutter in place. If the machine lifts while cutting, you might be cutting too many layers, or the material is not suitable for cutting. Remove a layer and try again.

Use a cutting mat that matches the size of die board being used. Cut with die blades running under the roller at an angle, not parallel to the roller, if possible. Align fabric to the edge of the shape being cut, not the edge of the die board. Refer to your GO! user's manual for other tips, and care and maintenance of the cutter and dies.

> ### Tip
>
> *Take care of your cutting mats. Store mats flat, out of direct sunlight and heat. Do not use a warped mat. Alternate mat sides when cutting to extend cutting life. Replace mats when cutting performance of dies is reduced or mat shows excessive wear.*

Be sure to read the entire user's manual before using your cutter. Never carry the GO! cutter in open position.

For questions about your AccuQuilt GO! Fabric Cutter, refer to your user's manual or contact AccuQuilt Customer Service at (888) 258-7913 or online at accuquilt.com.

> ### Tip
>
> *Test-cut one shape before cutting many shapes to ensure fabric orientation is correct.*

1 Place die on cutter, FOAM SIDE UP. Place fabric on top of die. ***Note:*** *To conserve fabric, cover only the shape you want to cut—not the entire die board. For asymmetrical shapes, place fabric pattern side up if you want the shape to look exactly like the shape on the die. Place fabric pattern side down if you want the shape to be a mirror image of the shape on the die.* Place cutting mat on top of fabric.

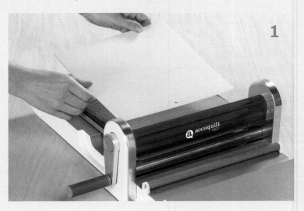

2 Push die, fabric and mat firmly against roller. Turn handle in direction you want the die to go.

3 Remove mat, die-cut shape and excess fabric. Add new fabric and cutting mat on top of die. Repeat process from opposite side. There is no need to handle the die between cuts!

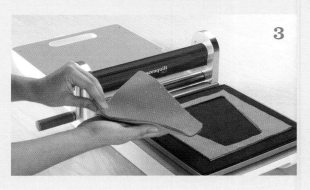

Fabric Reference Chart

Use this chart to determine the minimum fabric requirements needed to cut each GO!® fabric-cutting die shape listed.

Die Name (Item #)	Shape on Die	Layers of Cotton Fabric*	Precut Strip Size (width of fabric)	Fan-Fold Size	Cuts Per Precut Strip	Minimum Shapes Yielded Per 40" Usable-Width Yard Fabric	Helpful Hints
Geometric Shapes							
GO! Square—6½" (55000) (A)	Square	Up to 6	7½"	7½"	5	20	
GO! Square—3½" (55006) (B)	Squares	Up to 6	8"	4½"	16	72 or more	
GO! Triangle—6½" (55001) (C)	Triangles	Up to 6	7½"	7½"	10	40	
GO! Triangle—4⅞" (55002) (D)	Triangles	Up to 6	4½"		7	56	Open fabric strip out flat, layer fabric if desired, cut one set, and then continue to move strip over to cut across width of fabric.
GO! Half Square—3" Finished Triangle (55009) (E)	Half-Square Triangles	Up to 6	9½"	4½"	32 or more	128	For easy half-square triangles, layer fabrics right sides together on die and cut. Pick up one pair of triangles and sew.
GO! Square—4¾" (55019) (F)	Squares	Up to 6	10½"	5¾"	12 or more	36 or more	
GO! Parallelogram—3¾" W x 3½" H (55004) (G)	Parallelogram	Up to 6	3¾"		7	63	Open fabric strip out flat, layer fabric if desired, cut one shape, continue to move strip over to cut six more parallelograms across width of fabric. Layer fabric right sides together to cut pairs.
GO! Rectangle—3½" W x 6½" H (55005) (H)	Rectangle	Up to 6	7½"	4½"	8	32 or more	
Strip Cutter							
GO! Strip Cutter—2½" (55017)	Strips	Up to 6	8½" (for 3 strips), 25½" (for 9 strips)	8½"	3 per 8½"	12	Position fabric on die so folded edge goes through first.
Appliqué Shapes							
GO! Circle—2", 3", 5" (55012)	2" Circle	Up to 6; up to 4 prefused	3"	3"	13	156	
	3" Circle	Up to 6; up to 4 prefused	4"	4"	10	90	
	5" Circle	Up to 6; up to 4 prefused	6"	6"	6	36	
GO! Funky Flowers (55042)	Large Flowers	Up to 6; up to 4 prefused	5"	5"	8	56	
	Small Flowers	Up to 6; up to 4 prefused	2½"	2½"	16 or more	224 or more	
	Flower Centers	Up to 6; up to 4 prefused	Use scraps				

*Recommended layers of fabric are based on 100 percent cotton fabric. Number of layers of fabric varies by fabric type and thickness. Always begin with fewer layers and build up.

Fabric Guide for GO!

Fabric Type	Number of Layers*
Batik	Up to 6; up to 4 prefused
Cotton	Up to 6; up to 4 prefused
Denim	1
Felt	1
Flannel	Up to 2
Fleece	Up to 2
Ultrasuede	1
Wool	2

*Recommended Cutting Layers: The AccuQuilt GO!® Fabric Cutter cuts a wide variety of fabric in a varying number of layers. The number of layers you can cut depends on the type of material and the intricacy of the die. Always begin with fewer layers, and then build up. Often, more layers will improve cutting performance.

Basic Quiltmaking Techniques

Begin any quilting project by reading through all instructions. Like cooking, knowing what prep work needs to be done and gathering all the necessary "ingredients and tools" prior to starting, will make your quilting experience better.

There are several tools that every quilter needs in their sewing box (besides the AccuQuilt cutter and a sewing machine!). Basics include:

- Seam ripper
- Pincushion
- Hand-sewing needles and long, thin sharp pins
- Measuring tools
- Fabric-marking tools for dark and light fabrics
- Fabric scissors
- Iron and ironing surface
- Sewing machine needles sizes 75/11–80/12
- Ergonomic rotary cutter and at least an 18" self-healing cutting mat and 6" x 24" see-through quilting ruler

Prewashing fabrics is a personal choice. Some quilting cottons will shrink more and contain more residual dye than others. If washing, launder all fabrics you will be using. Don't mix washed and unwashed fabrics. Iron all fabrics before cutting.

Straighten your fabric yardage before doing any cutting. This will help you keep your fabric on grain when cutting. For best results when using the AccuQuilt cutter, try to lay fabrics on the die with the straight grain along a shape edge. Your fabric will cut better and the pieces will retain their shape while being sewn.

All projects in this book assume piecing with a ¼"-wide seam, sewn right sides together. Good pressing at each stage of block construction makes for a beautiful project. Set stitches by pressing seams flat. Specific pressing instructions will be noted in each pattern.

Finishing Your Quilt

After piecing the quilt top as instructed, finish your project with these easy steps:

Layer, Baste & Quilt

1. Mark quilting designs on the quilt top before layering with the batting and backing by tracing with a washable marking tool, using perforated paper patterns and chalk, or using purchased tear-away paper patterns. Some quilting designs—like meandering or stippling, outline, or stitch-in-the-ditch—do not require marking.

2. After ironing the backing, place it right side down on a clean, flat surface. For large projects, tape the edges of the backing to the floor or table using low-adhesive painter's tape, pulling it taut.

3. Place the batting on top of the backing, centering on the backing and smoothing out wrinkles.

4. Fold the quilt top in half lengthwise, right sides together, and lay centered on the batting. Unfold the quilt top and smooth over the batting (Figure 1). The batting and backing layers should be 3" to 8" larger than the quilt top, depending on the project's overall size.

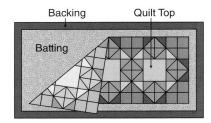

Figure 1

5. Baste the quilt layers together to prevent shifting during quilting. Hand-baste, safety-pin or spray-baste the quilt sandwich. If hand-basting or using safety pins, start in the center and move toward the outside edge using contrasting thread. If using a spray-basting product, consult the manufacturer's directions.

6. Quilt as desired by hand or machine; remove pins or basting thread if used. Trim excess backing and batting even with quilt top.

Binding Edges

When quilting is completed, binding finishes off and protects the quilt edges. The following instructions are for attaching a double-fold (also called a French fold) binding with mitered corners:

1. Overlap binding strips at right angles, right sides together. Sew across the diagonal and trim seam allowance to ¼", as seen in Figure 2. Press seams open. Join strips to make a length equal to the perimeter of the quilt plus at least 10".

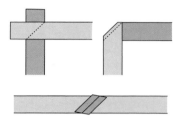

Figure 2

2. Fold ¼" to ½" of one end of the binding to the wrong side and press. Fold the strip in half lengthwise, wrong sides together and re-press referring to Figure 3.

Figure 3

3. Position the turned end of binding at least 12" from a corner. Then, matching raw edges of quilt top and binding, begin stitching binding to quilt top approximately 3" from the binding end, using a ¼" seam allowance (Figure 4). *Note: To have a filled binding that will wear well and look good, use a seam allowance that is approximately half the width of the folded binding. For example, for a binding cut 2½" wide and folded to 1¼" wide, use a seam allowance of ½" to ⅝".*

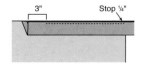

Figure 4

4. Sew binding to within ¼" (or your seam allowance) of the first corner; remove quilt from machine and trim threads. Fold the binding up at a 45-degree angle to the seam (Figure 5) and back down even with the quilt edges, forming a pleat at the corner (Figure 6). Resume stitching binding to the quilt top, sewing remaining corners as above.

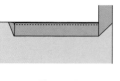

Figure 5

Figure 6

5. Stop sewing binding a short distance from the beginning tail of the binding. Remove the quilt from sewing machine and trim the end tail of the binding so that it tucks inside the beginning tail of the binding at least 2" (Figure 7). Resume stitching, sewing the binding tails to the quilt top, again referring to Figure 7.

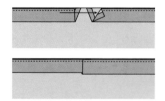

Figure 7

6. Turning binding to quilt back pulling over the seam line, stitch in place by hand or machine. Stitch a few stitches by hand in corners to close miters. ❖

Stepping Stones

Design by Julia Dunn

Cutting for this quilt happens even faster when you combine the AccuQuilt GO!® with 10-inch precut squares. You may be sleeping under this classy quilt by bedtime!

Project Note

Refer to AccuQuilt GO! die-cutting general instructions on page 3, for specific die-cutting processes.

Project Specifications

Skill Level: Beginner
Quilt Size: 82" x 106"
Block Size: 6" x 6"
Number of Blocks: 96 and 96

Half-Square
6" x 6" Block
Make 96

Four-Patch
6" x 6" Block
Make 96

Materials

- 2 Layer Cake™ bundles in coordinating rust, dark green, teal and olive
- 4 yards brown
- 5⅝ yards tan swirl
- Backing 90" x 114"
- Batting 90" x 114"
- Neutral-color all-purpose thread
- AccuQuilt GO! fabric cutter
- AccuQuilt dies:
    GO! Mix & Match B (55006) and C (55001)
    GO! Strip Cutter—2½" (55017)
- Basic quilting tools and supplies

Die-Cutting Instructions

1. Select 48 Layer Cake pieces. Fold each piece in half and die-cut 192 B squares.

2. Cut (12) 8" by fabric width strips tan swirl and fan-fold 4½" wide. Die-cut 192 B squares.

3. Cut (10) 7½" by fabric width strips tan swirl and fan-fold 7½" wide. Die-cut 96 C triangles.

4. Cut three 8½" by fabric width strips tan swirl and using the 2½" strip cutter, die-cut nine strips for I/J borders.

5. Cut (10) 7½" by fabric width strips brown and fan-fold 7½" wide. Die-cut 96 C triangles.

6. Cut three 8½" by fabric width strips brown and one 3½" by fabric width strip brown. Using the 2½" strip cutter, die-cut 10 strips for binding.

Additional Cutting Instructions

1. Cut (10) 3½" by fabric width strips brown for K/L borders.

Completing the Blocks

1. Sew a tan swirl B square to a Layer Cake B square (Figure 1). Press seam toward Layer Cake B square. Repeat to make 192 B/B units.

Figure 1

2. Sew two matching B/B units together to make a Four-Patch block referring to the block drawing. Press seam in one direction. Repeat to make 96 Four-Patch blocks.

3. Matching long edges, sew a tan swirl C triangle to a brown C triangle to make a Half-Square block (Figure 2). Press seam toward brown.

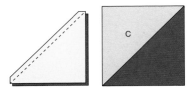

Figure 2

4. Repeat to make 96 Half-Square blocks.

Completing the Quilt

1. Choose 6 Four-Patch blocks and 6 Half-Square blocks. Referring to Figure 3, sew blocks together to make an X row. Press seams in one direction. Repeat to make 8 X rows referring to Placement Diagram for color placement.

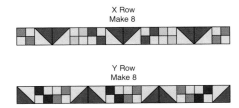

X Row
Make 8

Y Row
Make 8

Figure 3

2. From the remaining blocks, choose 6 each Four-Patch and Half-Square blocks. Again referring to Figure 3, sew blocks together to make a Y row. Press seams in opposite direction of X row. Repeat to make 8 Y rows.

3. Sew X and Y rows together to make 8 pairs of rows, referring to Figure 4.

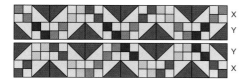

Figure 4

4. Sew two row pairs together matching Y row to Y row by reversing one pair as shown in Figure 5.

Figure 5

5. Continue adding row pairs matching X row to X row, then Y row to Y row as shown in Figure 6.

Figure 6

6. Sew J/I border strips together on short ends. Press seams open. Cut two I borders each 72½" and two J borders each 100½".

7. Referring to Placement Diagram, sew I borders to top and bottom of pieced center and J borders to sides.

Stepping Stones
Placement Diagram 82" x 106"

8. Sew K/L strips together on short ends. Press seams open. Cut two K borders each 76½" and two L borders each 106½".

9. Referring to Placement Diagram, sew K borders to top and bottom of pieced center and L borders to sides.

10. Layer, quilt and bind, with 2½" brown strips, following Finishing Your Quilt on page 6 of General Instructions. ❖

Tip

Purchasing and using precut 10" fabric squares eliminates having to cut fabric yardage and makes AccuQuilt quilting even quicker!

Waterfall

Designed & Quilted by Jill Reber

Watery aqua, blue and purple batiks set in the classic Shoo Fly block turns any bedroom into a soothing oasis. Soft yellow batiks create the look of the morning sun shimmering on water.

Project Note
Refer to AccuQuilt GO!® die-cutting general instructions on page 3, for specific die-cutting processes.

Project Specifications
Skill Level: Beginner
Quilt Size: 61" x 85"
Block Size: 9" x 9"
Number of Blocks: 24

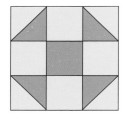

Shoo Fly
9" x 9" Block
Make 24

Materials
- 12 coordinating batik fat quarters in aquas, blues and purples
- 1⅞ yards light aqua batik
- 1⅞ yards dark aqua/purple batik
- 2⅓ yards light yellow batik
- Backing 69" x 93"
- Batting 69" x 93"
- Neutral-color all-purpose thread
- AccuQuilt GO! fabric cutter
- AccuQuilt dies:
    GO! Mix & Match B (55006) and E (55009)
- Basic quilting tools and supplies

Die-Cutting Instructions
1. Cut six 8" by fabric width strips light yellow batik and fan-fold 4½" wide. Die-cut 96 B squares.

2. Cut three 9½" by fabric width strips light yellow batik. Cut strips in half and fan-fold 4½" wide. Die-cut 96 E triangles.

3. Cut one 9½" by 22" strip from each of 12 coordinating fat quarter batiks and fan-fold 4½" wide. Die-cut 8 E triangles.

4. Cut one 8" by 22" strip from each of 12 coordinating fat quarter batiks and fan-fold 4½" wide. Die-cut 8 B squares.

5. From the coordinating fat quarter batik B and E pieces, group four E triangles and one B square into 24 matching sets. Keep 35 B squares for use as cornerstones in sashing. Set aside any extra B squares for another project.

Additional Cutting Instructions
1. Cut six 9½" by fabric width strips light aqua batik. Subcut strips into (58) 3½" x 9½" I rectangles.

2. Cut seven 5½" by fabric width strips dark aqua/purple batik for J/K borders.

3. Cut eight 2¼" by fabric width strips dark aqua/purple batik for binding.

Completing the Shoo Fly Block
1. Select a matching batik fabric set (prepared in step 5 above), four light yellow B squares and four light yellow E triangles.

2. Sew a light yellow batik and a fat quarter batik E triangle along long edge (Figure 1). Press seam toward darker batiks. Repeat to make four half-square units.

Figure 1

3. Matching darker edges of half-square unit to opposite sides of a light yellow B square, sew light yellow B square between two half-square units (Figure 2). Press seams toward square. Repeat to make top and bottom row of block.

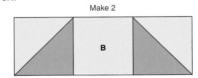

Figure 2

4. Sew matching fat quarter batik B square between two light yellow B squares to make block center row (Figure 3). Press seams toward light yellow B squares.

Figure 3

5. Sew rows together, referring to the Shoo Fly block diagram, pressing seams in one direction to complete Shoo Fly block.

6. Repeat steps 1–5 to make 24 Shoo Fly blocks.

Completing the Quilt

1. Sew four Shoo Fly blocks and five I sashing strips together in a row, alternating blocks and strips, and beginning and ending with I strips (Figure 4). Press seams toward I. Repeat to make six block rows.

Figure 4

2. Beginning with a fat quarter batik B square, sew four I sashing strips and five fat quarter batik B squares together alternately along short ends to make a sashing row (Figure 5). Press seams toward I. Repeat to make seven sashing rows.

Make 7

Figure 5

3. Sew sashing rows and block rows together alternately, beginning and ending with a sashing row as shown in Figure 6. Press seams in one direction.

Figure 6

4. Sew J/K strips together along short ends. Press seams open. Cut two 51½" J strips and two 85½" K strips.

5. Sew a J strip to the top and bottom of the pieced center and a K strip to each side referring to the Placement Diagram.

6. Layer, quilt and bind referring to Finishing Your Quilt on page 6 of General Instructions. ❖

Waterfall
Placement Diagram 61" x 85"

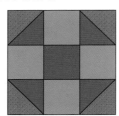

Bed of Roses

Design by Chris Malone
Quilted by June Macauley

Two traditional quilt blocks—the Snowball and the Shoo Fly—consist of identical pieces and layouts, yet create two distinctive blocks in this quilt.

Project Notes

All the Rose blocks can be cut from the same red print, or cut from gradually lighter shades in diagonal rows as shown. For a different look, go scrappy and use a wide variety of colors and prints.

Refer to AccuQuilt GO!® die-cutting general instructions on page 3, for specific die-cutting processes.

Project Specifications

Skill Level: Intermediate
Quilt Size: 81" x 99"
Block Size: 9" x 9"
Number of Blocks: 50 and 49

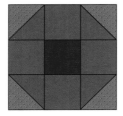

Shoo Fly
9" x 9" Block
Make 49

Rose
9" x 9" Block
Make 50

Materials

- Purchase a gradation of reds with R1 the darkest through to R10 the lightest:

⅛ yard R1	1 yard R6
⅓ yard R2	¾ yard R7
⅝ yard R3	⅝ yard R8
¾ yard R4	⅓ yard R9
1 yard R5	⅛ yard R10

- ⅞ yard dark red tonal for rose centers R11
- 3⅛ yards light green
- 3⅝ yards green/red floral
- 3⅝ yards dark green
- Backing 90" x 108"
- Batting 90" x 108"
- Neutral-color all-purpose thread
- AccuQuilt GO! fabric cutter
- AccuQuilt dies:
    GO! Mix & Match B (55006) and E (55009)
    GO! Strip Cutter—2½" (55017)
- Basic quilting tools and supplies

Die-Cutting Instructions

Green Fabrics

1. Cut four 8" by fabric width strips dark green and fan-fold 4½" wide. Die-cut 49 B squares.

2. Cut (13) 8" by fabric width strips light green and fan-fold 4½" wide. Die-cut 196 B squares.

3. Cut and layer, right sides together, seven 9½" by fabric width strips each green/red floral and dark green. Die-cut 196 E triangle pairs.

4. Cut six more 9½" by fabric width strips green/red floral. Fan-fold these strips along with the excess strip from step 3 into 4 ½"-wide folds. Die-cut 200 E triangles.

5. Cut one 25½" by fabric width strip dark green. With strip folded in half, fan-fold 8½" wide. Die-cut nine 2½" by fabric width strips using the strip cutter, for binding.

Red Fabrics

Notes: For fabrics R1, R2, R9 and R10, cut pieces as indicated. For other red fabrics cut strips and fan-fold 4½" wide for die cutting. Place matching B and E pieces in bags labeled by color (R1, R2, etc.).

1. Die-cut four B squares and four E triangles from both R1 and R10.

2. Die-cut 12 B squares and 12 E triangles from both R2 and R9.

3. Cut one 9½" by fabric width strip each from R3 and R8. Die-cut 20 E triangles from each strip. Cut one 8" by fabric width strip from both R3 and R8. Die-cut 16 B squares from each strip and four B squares individually from the remainder of the E triangle strip.

4. Cut two 8" by fabric width strips each from R4 and R7. Die-cut 28 B squares from each. Cut one 9½" by fabric width strip each from R4 and R7. Die-cut 28 E triangles from each strip.

5. Cut two 8" by fabric width strips each from R5 and R6. Die-cut 32 B squares from each. Cut one 9½" by fabric width strip each from R5 and R6. Die-cut 32 E triangles from each. Cut an extra four B squares and four E triangles individually from fabric excess to cut a total of 36 pieces each.

6. Cut three 8" by fabric width strips from R11. Die-cut 48 B squares. Die-cut two B squares individually from fabric excess to cut a total of 50 B squares.

Completing the Shoo Fly Block

1. Sew four pairs of dark green and green/red floral E triangles together along long edges. Press seams toward dark green, making four E/E half-square units (Figure 1).

Figure 1

2. Sew one E/E unit to each side of a light green B square with the green/red floral at the outside corners (Figure 2). Press seams toward B. Repeat to make two rows for top and bottom of block.

Figure 2

3. Sew a light green B square on either side of a dark green B square to create the center row (Figure 3). Press seams toward light green squares.

Figure 3

4. Referring to Shoo Fly block diagram, join the three rows to make a block.

5. Repeat steps 1–4 to make a total of 49 Shoo Fly blocks.

Completing the Rose Block

1. Using red group R1, sew four medium green/red floral E triangles, right sides together with four R1 E triangles to make four E/E half square units (Figure 4). Press seams toward medium green/red floral.

Figure 4   **Figure 5**

2. Sew one E/E unit to each side of an R1 B square with the green/red floral at the outside corner (Figure 5). Press seams toward E/E units. Repeat to make two rows for top and bottom of block.

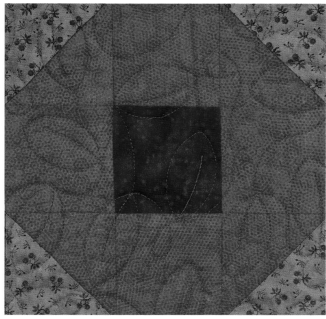

3. To make center row, sew one R1 B square to each side of an R11 B square; press seams toward R11 (Figure 6).

Figure 6

4. Referring to Rose block diagram, join the three rows together to make a block. Press seams toward center row.

5. Repeat steps 1–4 to make a total of 50 Rose blocks in the following combinations:

 1 each of R1 and R10

 3 each of R2 and R9

 5 each of R3 and R8

 7 each of R4 and R7

 9 each of R5 and R6

Note: Keep each group of blocks together and labeled with block numbers (R1, R2, etc.).

Completing the Quilt

1. Following Figure 7, sew blocks together in horizontal rows alternating Shoo Fly blocks and Rose blocks. Press seams toward Rose blocks.

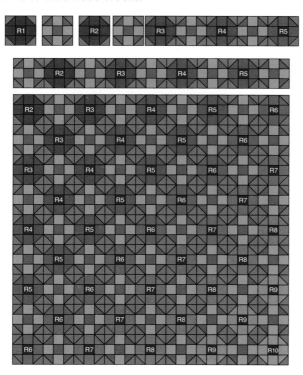

Figure 7

2. Sew rows together and press seams open to alleviate bulk.

3. Layer, quilt and bind referring to Finishing Your Quilt on page 6 of General Instructions. ❖

> ### Tip
>
> *When making half-square blocks from triangles, precut the strips from each color fabric needed. Layer the two coordinating strips right sides together and feed through the AccuQuilt cutter. Pick up each pair of triangles and sew.*
>
>   *—Chris Malone*

Bed of Roses
Placement Diagram 81" x 99"

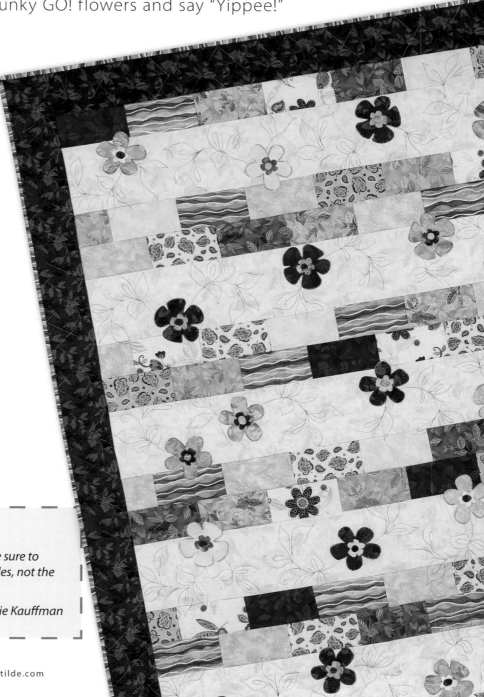

Bursting Into Bloom

Designed & Quilted by Connie Kauffman

This fun quilt couldn't be simpler. Sew wide strips with
bright- and bold-colored rectangle bricks to really pack a punch.
Add some Funky GO! flowers and say "Yippee!"

Project Note

Refer to AccuQuilt GO!® die-cutting
general instructions on page 3, for
specific die-cutting processes.

Project Specifications

Skill Level: Beginner
Quilt Size: 50" x 68"

Materials

- 1 fat quarter each 7 mottled fabrics,
  coordinated with bright prints
- ¼ yard each 5 coordinating bright prints
- 1 yard blue/green stripe
- 1⅛ yard dark blue print
- 1¼ yards light green tonal
- Backing 58" x 76"
- Batting 58" x 76"
- Neutral-color all-purpose thread
- Variegated thread
- 2 yards paper-backed fusible web
- Nonstick pressing sheet
- AccuQuilt GO! fabric cutter
- AccuQuilt dies:
  GO! Mix & Match H (55005)
  GO! Funky Flowers (55042)
  GO! Strip Cutter—2½" (55017)
- Basic quilting tools and supplies

Tip

*If fabric has a stripe or directional print, be sure to
lay it straight with the edge of the die blades, not the
edge of the die board.*

—*Connie Kauffman*

House of White Birches, Berne, Indiana 46711   Clotilde.com

Die-Cutting Instructions

1. Cut one 7½" by fabric width strip from each of five coordinating bright prints and fan-fold 4½" wide. Die-cut eight H rectangles from each strip.

2. Cut one 7½" x 22" width strip from each of seven mottled fat quarters, coordinated with prints, and fan-fold 4½" wide. Die-cut four H rectangles from each strip.

3. Cut one 7½" by fabric width strip blue/green stripe and fan-fold 4½" wide. Die-cut eight H rectangles.

4. Cut two 8½" by fabric width strip and one 3½" by fabric width strip from blue/green stripe and fan-fold 4½" wide. Using the 2½" strip cutter, die-cut seven 2½" by fabric width strips for binding.

Additional Cutting Instructions

1. Cut seven 4½" by fabric width strips dark blue print for K/L borders.

2. Cut six 6½" by fabric width strips light green tonal for J.

3. Choose eight different H rectangles and trim to 3½" x 3½" for I.

Preparing Appliqué

1. Choose a variety of scraps at least 5" x 5" from the coordinating bright prints and mottleds, blue/green stripe and the dark blue. Apply paper-backed fusible web to the back of each piece.

2. Using the Funky Flowers AccuQuilt GO! die and following general instructions on page 3, individually cut 20 each of the large flowers, small flowers and flower centers from the prepared scrap fabrics in contrasting colors, referring to sample photos. *Note: If you are using the flower templates on page 24, trace 20 of each large flowers, small flowers and flower centers onto the paper side of the paper-backed fusible web leaving ½" between shapes. Cut out shapes leaving ¼" around each. Following the manufacturer's instructions, apply shapes to the wrong side of fabric for flowers. Trim on traced line for flower appliqués.*

3. Remove paper backing from small flowers and centers. Arrange contrasting small flowers on large flowers and center contrasting flower centers on small flowers (Figure 1).

Figure 1

4. Using a nonstick pressing sheet to protect your iron surface, fuse flowers together following manufacturer's instructions. Set flowers aside.

Completing the Quilt

1. Choose a variety of 42 H rectangles and group into six groups of seven rectangles each.

2. Varying the placement, sew each group of H rectangles together on short ends to make six X rows (Figure 2). Press seams in same direction.

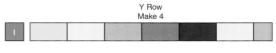

X Row
Make 6

Figure 2

3. Choose a variety of 24 H rectangles and make four rows of six rectangles each in the same manner as step 2. Sew an I square to both ends of the rows to make four Y rows (Figure 3). Press seams in same direction.

Y Row
Make 4

Figure 3

Tip

Use coordinating scraps, fat quarters or smaller yardages to individually cut appliqué shapes.

4. Sew the J strips together on short ends, press seams open. Cut into five J strips 42½" long.

5. Sew an X row to both long edges of a J strip (Figure 4). Press seams toward J.

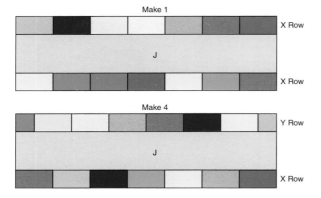

Figure 4

6. Sew a Y row to the top of a J strip and an X row to the bottom. Press seams toward J. Make four Y/J/X rows again referring to Figure 4.

7. Remove the backing from the fused flowers and arrange four different flowers on each J strip referring to Placement Diagram or photo. Vary flower placement, with some flowers overlapping into the H rectangles. Fuse flowers in place.

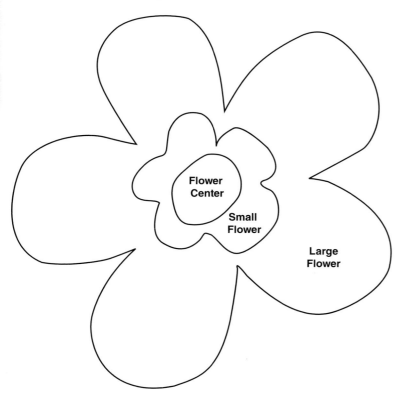

8. Using a buttonhole stitch and coordinating variegated thread, stitch around each large and small flower and flower center.

9. Sew a Y/J/X row to the bottom of the X/J/X row. Add three more Y/J/X rows, referring to Figure 5, to complete the quilt center.

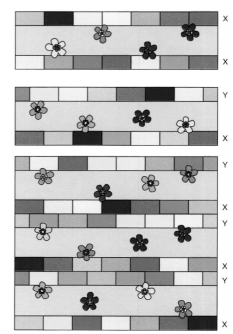

Figure 5

10. Sew the K/L border strips together at short ends, press seams open. Cut into two 42½" K strips and two 68½" L strips.

11. Sew K strips to the top and bottom of quilt center and L strips to long sides.

12. Layer and quilt following Finishing Your Quilt on page 6 of General Instructions. ***Note:*** *In this quilt, the designer used variegated thread to quilt a leafy vine pattern around the flowers in the center of the quilt and on the border corners. Remaining borders have crosshatch stitching.*

13. Bind using the blue/green stripe 2½" strips and following Binding Edges on page 7 of General Instructions. ❖

Bursting Into Bloom
Placement Diagram 50" x 68"

Flash of Lightning

Designed & Quilted by Julie Weaver

Who knew such a "striking" quilt could be made from just four coordinating fabrics? A lack of sashing creates the look of lightning across the center of this youthful quilt.

Project Note

Refer to AccuQuilt GO!® die-cutting general instructions on page 3, for specific die-cutting processes.

Project Specifications

Skill Level: Beginner
Quilt Size: 48" x 60"
Block Size: 12" x 12"
Number of Blocks: 6 and 6

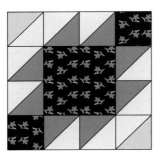

Blue
12" x 12" Block
Make 6

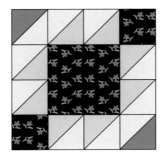

Yellow
12" x 12" Block
Make 6

Materials

- ⅔ yard yellow print
- ⅔ yard blue print
- 1⅛ yards small brown print
- 1⅓ yards brown floral print
- 1⅔ yards cream print
- Backing 52" x 64"
- Batting 52" x 64"
- Neutral-color all-purpose thread
- AccuQuilt GO! fabric cutter
- AccuQuilt dies:
    GO! Mix & Match A (55000), B (55006) and E (55009)
    GO! Strip Cutter—2½" (55017)
- Basic quilting tools and supplies

Die-Cutting Instructions

1. Cut three 7½" by fabric width strips small brown print and fan-fold 7½" wide. Die-cut 12 A squares.

2. Cut two 8" by fabric width strips small brown print and fan-fold 4½" wide. Die-cut 24 B squares.

3. Cut two 9½" by fabric width strips yellow print and fan-fold 4½" wide. Die-cut 60 E triangles.

4. Cut two 9½" by fabric width strips blue print and fan-fold 4½" wide. Die-cut 60 E triangles.

5. Cut four 9½" by fabric width strips cream print and fan-fold 4½" wide. Die-cut 120 E triangles.

6. Cut two 8½" by fabric width strips cream print. Die-cut five 2½" strips using strip cutter for I/J borders.

7. Cut two 8½" by fabric width strips small brown print. Die-cut six 2½" strips using strip cutter for binding.

Additional Cutting Instructions

1. Cut six 4½" by fabric width strips for K/L borders from the brown floral print.

Completing the Quilt

1. Sew the yellow print E triangles to 60 cream print E triangles. Press seams toward yellow. Repeat with 60 blue print and cream print triangles, to make 60 each yellow/cream and blue/cream E/E squares (Figure 1).

Figure 1

2. Referring to Figure 2, sew one blue/cream E/E square, two yellow/cream E/E squares and one B square together to make an X row. Repeat to make 12 X rows.

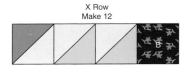

X Row
Make 12

Figure 2

3. Referring to Figure 3, sew 2 yellow/cream E/E squares together. Repeat to make 12 sets.

Figure 3

4. Sew yellow/cream sets to either side of one A square to make a Y row as shown in Figure 4. Repeat to make six Y rows.

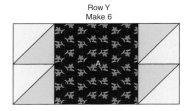

Row Y
Make 6

Figure 4

5. Sew a Y row between two X rows, referring to Yellow block diagram for orientation, to make a Yellow block. Repeat to make six Yellow blocks.

6. Repeat steps 2–4, using 48 blue/cream E/E squares, 12 yellow/cream E/E squares, 12 B squares and six A squares to make six Blue blocks, referring to block diagram for orientation.

7. Referring to Figure 5, sew a Blue block between two Yellow blocks. Repeat to make two yellow rows.

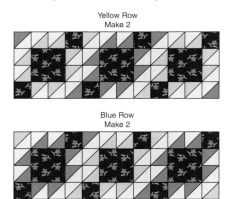

Yellow Row
Make 2

Blue Row
Make 2

Figure 5

8. Again referring to Figure 5, sew a Yellow block between two Blue blocks. Repeat to make two blue rows.

9. Beginning with a yellow row, sew the rows together alternately, referring to the Placement Diagram.

10. Sew the I/J strips together on short ends. Press seams open. Subcut into two 48½" I borders and two 40½" J borders. Sew I to sides and J to top and bottom of quilt center. Press seams toward borders.

11. Sew the K/L strips together on short ends. Press seams open. Subcut into two 52½" K borders and two 48½" L borders. Sew K to sides and L to top and bottom of quilt center. Press seams toward K and L.

12. Layer, quilt and bind, with the 2½" small brown print strips, following the Finishing Your Quilt on page 6 of General Instructions. ❖

> ### Tip
>
> *You will have extra cut shapes left over when finished. Save them to use for pillows, shams, bags, etc. The nice thing about using the AccuQuilt GO! cutter and dies is that what you have left is cut, usable and ready to GO! for your next project!*
>
> —*Julie Weaver*

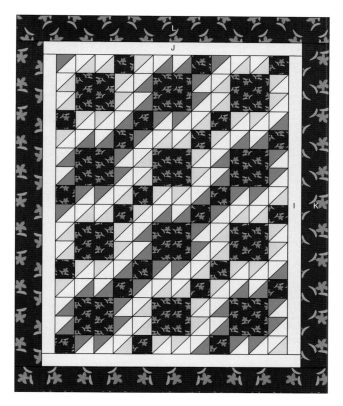

Flash of Lightning
Placement Diagram 48" x 60"

Garden Trellis

Design by Julie Weaver
Quilted by Twyla Voldseth

The wide sashing in this quilt adds interest and depth—are the blocks the story, or is it the sashing? Either way, this quilt is a showstopper.

Project Note

Refer to AccuQuilt GO!® die-cutting general instructions on page 3, for specific die-cutting processes.

Project Specifications

Skill Level: Advanced
Quilt Size: 90" x 108"
Block Size: 12" x 12"
Number of Blocks: 20

Strip
12" x 12" Block
Make 20

Materials

- 20 coordinating fat quarters
- 1⅓ yards red stripe print
- 2 yards red tone-on-tone print
- 2½ yards small floral print
- 4½ yards large floral print
- Backing 98" x 116"
- Batting 98" x 116"
- Neutral-color all-purpose thread
- AccuQuilt GO! fabric cutter
- AccuQuilt dies:
    GO! Mix & Match A (55000), E (55009) and H (55005)
    GO! Strip Cutter—2½" (55017)
- Basic quilting tools and supplies

Die-Cutting Instructions

1. Fold each fat quarter in half lengthwise (9" x 22") and die-cut six strips using the 2½"-strip cutter. *Note: Folded edge of fabric will not go through cutter first.* From each six-strip group, cut three 2½" x 12½" I rectangles and six 2½" x 6½" J rectangles for a total of 60 I and 120 J rectangles.

2. Cut (10) 8½" by fabric width strips small floral print. Using the 2½"-strip cutter, die-cut 28 K strips.

3. Cut four 8½" by fabric width strips red stripe. Using the 2½"-strip cutter, die-cut 11 L strips.

4. Cut four 8½" by fabric width strips large floral print. Using the 2½"-strip cutter, die-cut 11 strips for binding.

5. Cut three 7½" by fabric width strips large floral print and fan-fold 7½" wide. Die-cut 12 A squares.

6. Cut two 7½" by fabric width strips large floral print and fan-fold 4½" wide. Die-cut 14 H rectangles.

7. Cut five 9½" by fabric width strips red tone-on-tone print and fan-fold 4½" wide. Die-cut 160 E triangles.

Additional Cutting Instructions

1. Cut six 1½" by fabric width strips red stripe for N border strips.

2. Cut nine 2" by fabric width strips red tone-on-tone print for O/P border strips.

3. Cut four 3½" M squares from large floral print.

4. Cut (10) 8" by fabric width strips large floral print for Q/R border strips.

Completing the Strip Block

1. Choose three different-color I strips and sew together along long sides (Figure 1), to make an I unit; press seams in one direction.

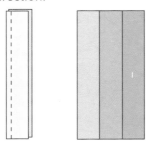

Figure 1

2. Choose six J strips and sew together along long sides (Figure 2), to make a J unit; press seams in one direction.

Figure 2

3. Sew long sides of I and J units together referring to Strip block diagram. Press seam toward I unit.

4. Repeat steps 1–3 to make 20 Strip blocks.

Completing Pieced Sashing Units

1. Sew a K strip on either side of an L strip. Repeat to make 11 K/L strip sets. Press seams toward K.

2. Subcut each strip set into three 12½" lengths (Figure 3). Repeat to make 31 K/L units.

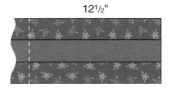
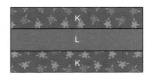

Figure 3

3. Sew an E triangle to one corner of a K/L unit as shown in Figure 4. Trim K/L corner even with seam allowance (Figure 4) and press seam toward E. Repeat on remaining corners (Figure 5) to create a pieced sashing unit.

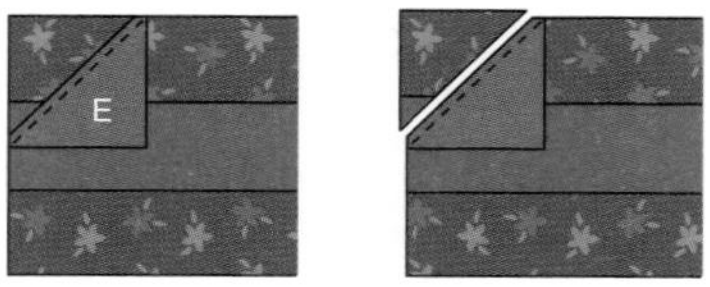

Figure 4

Figure 5

4. Repeat step 3 to make 31 pieced sashing units.

Completing Pieced Border

1. Sew a K strip to an N strip along long side. Press seam toward K. Repeat to make six K/N strip sets.

2. Subcut each strip set into three 12½" lengths to make 18 K/N units (Figure 6).

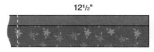

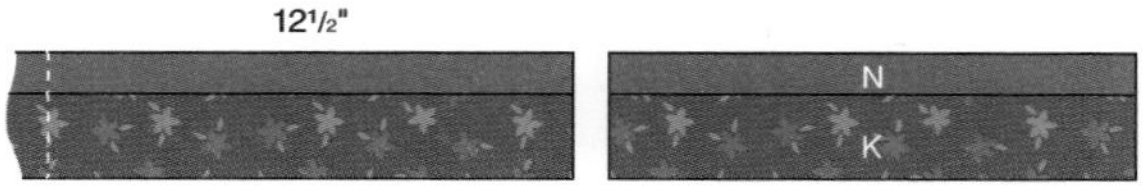

12½"

Figure 6

3. Sew an E triangle to the K corners of the K/N units, referring to Figure 7 and step 3 of Completing Pieced Sashing Units.

Figure 7

4. Repeat step 3 to make 18 K/N/E units.

5. To make top pieced border, sew three H rectangles and four K/N/E units together in a row referring to Figure 8. Repeat to make bottom border.

6. To make side pieced borders; sew two M squares, five K/N/E units and four H rectangles together in a row referring to Figure 8. Repeat to make two side borders.

Make 2

Make 2

Figure 8

Completing the Center

1. Sew three pieced sashing units between four Strip blocks to make an X row, turning Strip blocks alternately as shown in Figure 9. Press seams toward Strip blocks. Repeat to make three rows.

X Row
Make 3

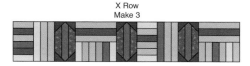

Figure 9

2. Sew three pieced sashing units between four Strip blocks to make a Y row as shown in Figure 10. Press seams toward Strip blocks. Repeat to make two rows.

Y Row
Make 2

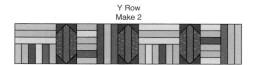

Figure 10

3. Sew three A squares between four pieced sashing units referring to Figure 11. Press seams toward A. Repeat to make four sashing rows.

Make 4

Figure 11

4. Referring to Figure 12 for row placement, stitch sashing and block rows together to complete quilt center. Press seams in one direction.

Figure 12

Completing the Quilt

1. Sew top and bottom pieced borders with K side toward center and referring to Placement Diagram, to short edges of quilt center. Press seam toward border.

2. Sew side borders, with K side toward center and referring to Placement Diagram, to long sides of quilt center. Press seam toward border.

3. Sew O/P strips together along short ends. Press seams open. Cut two 90½" O strips and two 75½" P strips.

4. Sew O strips to sides of quilt and P strips to top and bottom.

5. Sew Q/R strips together along short ends. Press seams open. Cut two 93½" Q strips and two 90½" R strips.

6. Sew Q strips along sides of quilt and R strips to top and bottom.

7. Layer, quilt and bind, with the 2½" x fabric width large floral print strips, following Finishing Your Quilt on page 6 in General Instructions. ❖

Tip

To position fabric for cutting strips from the 2½" strip die, bring the folded edge of the fabric to the selvage edge and press. I found that pressing the fabric before positioning it on the die helps ease out any wrinkles that could show up in the finished cuts.

—Julie Weaver

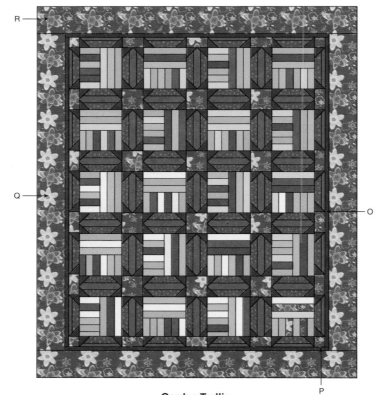

Garden Trellis
Placement Diagram 90" x 108"

Points of Interest

Designed & Quilted by Connie Kauffman

Fold simple die-cut shapes to create dimension. Prairie points add interest and create movement in this earthy, yet elegant, table topper.

Project Note

Refer to AccuQuilt GO! die-cutting general instructions on page 3, for specific die-cutting processes.

Project Specifications

Skill Level: Intermediate
Quilt Size: 24" x 24"
Block Size: 6" x 6"
Number of Blocks: 8 and 4

Block 1
6" x 6" Block
Make 8

Block 2
6" x 6" Block
Make 4

Materials

- ⅜ yard tan batik
- ½ yard turquoise batik
- ½ yard orange batik
- 1⅝ yards brown batik
- Batting 28" x 28"
- Neutral-color all-purpose thread
- Variegated quilting thread
- AccuQuilt GO! fabric cutter
- AccuQuilt dies:
  GO! Mix & Match B (55006), C (55001), E (55009) and F (55019)
- 1 (1⅛") brown button
- 12 (⅜") teal buttons
- Basic quilting tools and supplies

Die-Cutting Instructions

1. Cut one 8" by fabric width strip of brown batik and fan-fold 4½" wide. Die-cut 16 B squares.

2. Cut one 8" x 11" strip orange batik and fan-fold 4½" wide. Die-cut four B squares.

3. Cut one 8" x 23" strip tan batik and fan-fold 4½" wide. Die-cut eight B squares.

4. Cut one 7½" by fabric width strip brown batik and fan-fold 7½" wide. Die-cut eight C triangles.

5. Cut one 7½" by fabric width strip turquoise batik and fan-fold 7½" wide. Die-cut four C triangles.

6. Cut one 9½" x 18" strip of brown batik and fan-fold 4½" wide. Die-cut 16 E triangles.

7. Cut one 9½" x 9" strip orange batik and fan-fold 4½" wide. Die-cut eight E triangles.

8. Cut one 9½" x 9" strip tan batik and fan-fold 4½" wide. Die-cut eight E triangles.

9. Cut one 10½" x 9" strip orange batik and fan-fold 5¾" wide. Die-cut four F squares.

10. Cut one 10½" x 9" strip turquoise batik and fan-fold 5¾" wide. Die-cut four F squares.

Additional Cutting Instructions

1. From brown batik cut a 28" x 28" square for backing.

Making Small Prairie Points

1. Fold and press orange and tan B squares in half on both diagonals, referring to Figure 1. Make four orange and eight tan prairie points.

Figure 1

2. Lay an orange prairie point between two tan points, overlapping edges as shown in Figure 2. Adjust positioning so that there is 1½" between triangle points as shown in Figure 2. Pin and baste through all points.

Figure 2

3. Trim excess ¼" below basting (Figure 3).

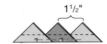

Figure 3

Repeat steps 1 and 2 to make four sets of small prairie points. Set aside. ***Note:*** *Pay close attention to the direction of the folded triangles, it looks nice to have all folded edges going in the same direction in each set. To do this, keep prairie points organized and aligned in sets as you fold and press.*

Making the Blocks

1. Sew a brown E triangle to a tan E triangle along long edge (Figure 4). Press seam toward brown E. Repeat with a brown E triangle and an orange E triangle. Make eight of each color E/E squares (Figure 4).

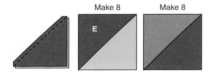

Figure 4

2. Sew an E/E square to a brown B square. Repeat with all E/E squares, making eight B/E tan and B/E orange units (Figure 5).

Figure 5

3. Sew a B/E tan unit to a B/E orange unit, referring to Block 1 diagram, to make eight Block 1 blocks. Referring to Figure 6, sew blocks together in (four) two-block units.

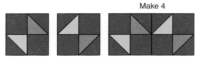

Figure 6

4. Using four each turquoise and orange F squares, fold squares in half on both diagonals and press to make a large prairie point, referring to Figure 1. Make four each orange and turquoise large prairie points.

5. Center and baste a large prairie point on each brown C triangle (Figure 7). ***Note:*** *Turquoise points will lie flat on C triangles until project is turned right side out before quilting, when they will extend out from project corners.*

Figure 7

6. Sew turquoise C triangles to brown C triangles with orange prairie points, referring to Figure 8. Press seam toward brown C triangles. Repeat to make four C units.

Figure 8

7. Center and baste a set of small prairie points on the turquoise side of C units, as shown in Figure 9, to complete a Block 2. Repeat to make four Block 2 blocks.

Figure 9

8. Referring to Figure 10 for orientation, sew four completed Block 2 blocks together to make the center unit.

Figure 10

Completing the Quilt

1. Sew a turquoise prairie point C triangle to either side of a Block 1 unit (Figure 11). Press seams toward C triangles. Repeat to make a top and bottom row. Sew a Block 1 unit to either side of the center unit to make

Tip

Press the fabric before positioning it on the die to eliminate any wrinkles that could show up in the finished cuts.

center row, referring to Figure 11. Press seams toward center unit.

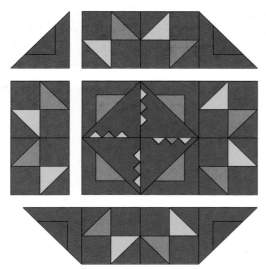

Figure 11

2. Sew top and bottom rows to the center row, again referring to Figure 11 for placement and orientation. Press seams in one direction.

3. Layer 28" x 28" batting, 28" x 28" backing piece, right side up; and the completed quilt top, right side down, on a flat surface and pin or baste around outside edge of quilt sandwich through all layers. *Note: Make sure turquoise triangles are folded toward quilt center.*

Tip

Don't waste that fabric! For easy scrap quilts, take all your project scraps and cut them into individual shapes before putting away your GO! cutter. Store the shapes in shoe boxes labeled with the type of shape in the box. The next time you need a scrap quilt, pull out the appropriate boxes and start stitching.

4. Sew ¼" around quilt sandwich outside edges, leaving a 4" opening for turning.

5. Trim batting and backing to match quilt top and turn right side out through opening.

6. Press edges, turning opening seam allowance to inside. Press turquoise points away from quilt center. Hand-stitch opening closed. Quilt as desired.

7. Finish quilt by sewing large button at quilt center and 3 small buttons on each side, extending out from turquoise center corners as seen in Placement Diagram and project photo. ❖

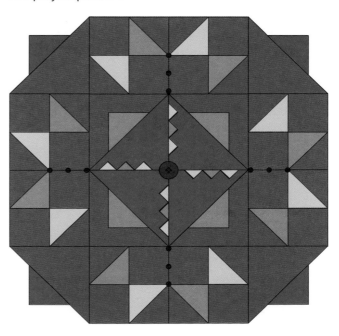

Points of Interest
Placement Diagram 24" x 24"

Imperial Gardens Place Mats

Designed & Quilted by Jill Reber

A set of elegant place mats comes together easily in an afternoon when using the AccuQuilt GO!® cutter. Add some style to your dinner table tonight, or make a quick set for a friend.

Project Notes

Materials listed and instructions are for two place mats.

Refer to AccuQuilt GO!® die-cutting general instructions on page 3, for specific die-cutting processes.

Project Specifications

Skill Level: Beginner
Place Mat Size: 14" x 20"
Block Size: 6" x 6"
Number of Blocks: 4 and 4

Light
6" x 6" Block
Make 4

Medium
6" x 6" Block
Make 4

Materials

- 2 fat quarters medium purple
- 2 fat quarters light purple
- ¼ yard green print
- 1½ yard dark purple
- 2 pieces 18" x 24" batting
- Neutral-color all-purpose thread
- AccuQuilt GO! fabric cutter
- AccuQuilt dies:
    GO! Mix & Match B (55006), D (55002), E (55009) and H (55005)
- Basic quilting tools and supplies

Die-Cutting Instructions

1. Cut one 9½" by fabric width strip dark purple and fan-fold 4½" wide. Die-cut 16 E triangles.

2. Cut one 7½" by fabric width strip dark purple and fan-fold 4½" wide. Die-cut eight H rectangles.

3. Cut one 8" by 22" strip from each medium and light purple fat quarter. Die-cut four B squares from each strip.

4. Cut two 4½" x 22" strips from each medium and light purple fat quarter. Die-cut four D triangles from each strip.

Additional Cutting Instructions

1. Cut one 6½" by fabric width strip dark purple. Subcut into two I rectangles 6½" x 12½".

2. Cut two 18" x 24" rectangles dark purple for place mat backing.

3. Cut four 1½" by fabric width strips from green print for borders. Subcut four 1½" x 12½" J borders and four 1½" x 20½" K borders.

4. Cut four 2½" x 22" strips from light and medium purple for binding.

Completing the Place Mats

1. Sew a dark purple E triangle to both sides of a light D triangle (Figure 1). Press seams toward E. Repeat to make four light purple flying geese units.

Figure 1

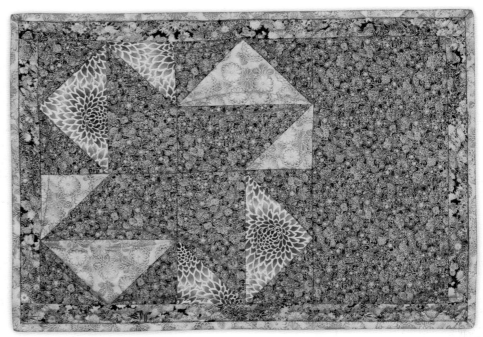

2. Repeat step 1 with medium purple D triangles and dark purple E triangles to make four medium purple flying geese units.

3. Use a ruler to draw a diagonal line on the wrong side of each B square. Sew a B square to the left corner of each H rectangle stitching on diagonal line, referring to Figure 2. Trim seam to ¼" and press toward B (Figure 2). Repeat to make four light purple B/H units and 4 medium B/H units.

Figure 2

4. Sew a light flying geese unit and light B/H unit together along one long edge, referring to Figure 3. Press seams toward B/H unit. Using light and medium purple units, make four Light blocks and four Medium blocks.

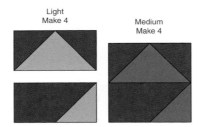

Figure 3

5. Sew a Light and Medium block together, referring to Figure 4 for orientation. Repeat to make four rows, two for each place mat.

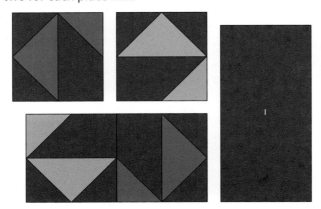

Figure 4

6. Sew two rows together for each place mat, again referring to Figure 4 for orientation of rows, to make two block units.

7. Sew I to the right side of each block unit, again referring to Figure 4. Press seams toward I.

8. Sew J borders to sides and K borders to top and bottom of place mat. Press seams toward borders. Repeat for second place mat.

9. Layer, quilt and bind, using the light and medium purple 2½" strips, following Finishing Your Quilt on page 6 of General Instructions. *Note: Use medium purple strips for one place mat and light purple strips for second place mat.* ❖

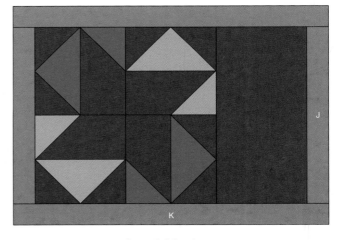

Imperial Gardens
Placement Diagram 14" x 20"

Hidden Stars

Design by Julia Dunn

Fall asleep under the stars. Combine Flying Geese with Four-Patch units to create the classic Eight-Pointed Star design.

Project Note

Refer to AccuQuilt GO!® die-cutting general instructions on page 3, for specific die-cutting processes.

Project Specifications

Skill Level: Confident beginner
Quilt Size: 78" x 102"
Block Size: 6" x 6"
Number of Blocks: 83 and 82

Four-Patch
6" x 6" Block
Make 83

Flying Geese
6" x 6" Block
Make 82

Materials

- 2 yards navy blue mottled
- 2⅝ yards total rose print
- 2⅝ yards total federal blue print
- 2⅝ yards burgundy mottled
- 4 yards cream mottled
- Backing 86" x 110"
- Batting 86" x 110"
- Neutral-color all-purpose thread
- AccuQuilt GO! fabric cutter
- AccuQuilt dies:
    GO! Mix & Match B (55006), D (55002),
    E (55009) and H (55005)
    GO! Strip Cutter—2½" (55017)
- Basic quilting tools and supplies

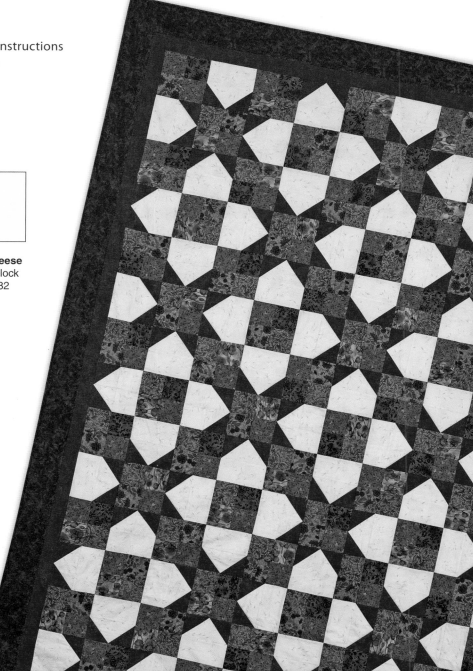

Die-Cutting Instructions

1. Cut (11) 8" by fabric width strips rose print and fan-fold 4½" wide. Die-cut 166 B squares. ***Note:*** *If using smaller cuts of fabric or scraps, die-cut B squares individually or with strips 8" wide, according to fabric piece size.*

2. Cut (11) 8" by fabric width strips federal blue print and fan-fold 4½" wide. Die-cut 166 B squares.

3. Cut (12) 4½" by fabric width strips cream mottled, layer strips and die-cut 82 D triangles.

4. Cut six 9½" strips by fabric width burgundy mottled and fan-fold 4½" wide. Die-cut 164 E triangles.

5. Cut (11) 7½" by fabric width cream mottled and fan-fold 4½" wide. Die-cut 82 H rectangles.

6. Cut one 25½" x fabric width strip burgundy mottled. With strip folded in half, fan-fold in 8½"-wide folds. Using the 2½" strip cutter, die-cut 9 strips for I/J borders.

7. Cut one 25½" x fabric width strip navy mottled. With strip folded in half, fan-fold in 8½"-wide folds. Using the 2½" strip cutter, die-cut 9 strips for binding.

Additional Cutting Instructions

1. Cut nine 4½" x fabric width strips navy blue mottled for K/L borders.

Completing the Four-Patch Blocks

1. Sew a federal blue B square to a rose B square. Press seam toward federal blue. Repeat to make 166 B/B units (Figure 1).

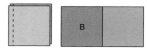

Figure 1

2. Sew B/B units together matching blue squares to rose squares to make 83 Four-Patch blocks (Figure 2). Press seams open to avoid bulk.

Figure 2

Completing the Flying Geese Blocks

1. Sew a burgundy mottled E triangle to both sides of a D cream mottled triangle as shown in Figure 3. Press seams toward E. Repeat to make 82 flying geese units.

Figure 3

2. Sew the long cream edge of a flying geese unit to a long edge of a cream H rectangle (Figure 4). Press seam open to avoid bulk.

Figure 4

3. Repeat to make 82 Flying Geese blocks.

Completing the Quilt

1. Select six Four-Patch blocks and five Flying Geese blocks. Beginning with a Four-Patch block, lay out blocks, referring to Figure 5. Sew blocks together to make W row; press seams open to avoid bulk. Repeat to make a total of four W rows, referring to Figure 5.

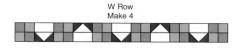

Figure 5

2. Sew X row in the same manner as W row, using six Flying Geese blocks and five Four-Patch blocks referring to Figure 6 for placement. Repeat to make a total of four X rows.

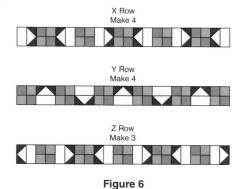

Figure 6

3. Sew Y rows in the same manner as W row, using six Four-Patch blocks and five Flying Geese blocks again referring to Figure 6. Repeat to make a total of four Y rows.

4. Sew Z row in the same manner as W row, using six Flying Geese blocks and five Four-Patch blocks again referring to Figure 6. Repeat to make a total of three Z rows.

5. Sew rows together in order shown in Figure 7, matching seams. Press seams open to avoid bulk.

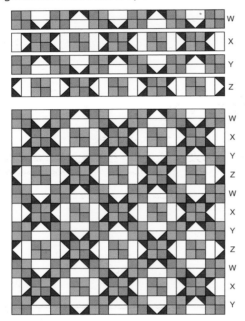

Figure 7

6. Sew I/J strips together at short ends; press seams open. Cut into two 66½" I border strips and two 94½" J border strips.

7. Sew I borders to top and bottom of pieced center and J borders to sides, referring to Placement Diagram.

8. Sew K/L strips together at short ends; press seams open. Cut into two 70½" K border strips and two 102½" L border strips.

9. Sew K borders to top and bottom of pieced center and L borders to sides, referring to Placement Diagram.

10. Layer, quilt and bind with navy mottled 2½" strips following Finishing Your Quilt on page 6 of General Instructions. ❖

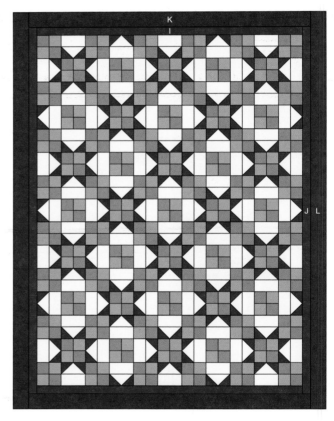

Hidden Stars
Placement Diagram 78" x 102"

Tip

Set up the cutter on a sturdy table with ample space to work and lay out fabric. As you cut, label pieces and place in a project box.

Row House Bed Runner

Designed & Quilted by Chris Malone

A quaint Nine-Patch neighborhood adorns this quirky, comforting bed runner. Stacked Flying Geese create the trees.

Project Note

Refer to AccuQuilt GO!® die-cutting general instructions on page 3, for specific die-cutting processes.

Project Specifications

Skill Level: Beginner
Quilt Size: 83" x 21"
Block Sizes: 6" x 15" and 12" x 15"
Number of Blocks: 4 and 4

House
12" x 15" Block
Make 4

Tree
6" x 15" Block
Make 4

Materials

- Scrap dark brown print
- 9 (8" x 9") pieces coordinating prints
- 4 light green to dark green fat quarter prints
- ¼ yard brown floral
- ⅝ yard green paisley
- ⅞ yard brown print
- 1 yard blue/green dot
- Backing 90" x 27"
- Batting 90" x 27"
- Neutral-color all-purpose thread
- Ecru size 12 pearl cotton (or hand-quilting thread)
- 4 tan ¾" buttons
- 21 green ¾" buttons
- AccuQuilt GO! fabric cutter
- AccuQuilt dies:
    GO! Mix & Match B (55006), C (55001), D (55002) and E (55009)
    GO! Strip Cutter—2½" (55017)
- Basic quilting tools and supplies

Die-Cutting Instructions

1. Fold each 8" x 9" piece of the nine coordinating prints in half to 8" x 4½" and layer the pieces to cut. Die-cut four B squares from each print.

2. Cut one 7½" by fabric width strip blue/green dot and fan-fold 7½" wide. Die-cut eight C triangles.

3. Cut one 7½" by fabric width strip brown floral and fan-fold 7½" wide. Die-cut eight C triangles.

4. Cut one 4½" x 22" strip from each of the four green prints. Layer the strips and die-cut four D triangles.

5. Cut one 9½" by fabric width strip blue/green dot and fan-fold 4½" wide. Die-cut 32 E triangles.

6. Cut one 25½" x fabric width strip brown print and fan-fold 8½" wide. Die-cut nine 2½" strips using the strip cutter. Set seven strips aside for binding.

7. Cut two 8½" by fabric width strip green paisley and fan-fold 8½" wide. Die-cut six 2½" strips using the strip cutter.

Additional Cutting Instructions

1. Cut two 2" by fabric width strips blue/green dot. Subcut into eight 9½" I strips.

2. Cut one 3" by fabric width strip blue/green dot. Subcut into eight 3½" K strips.

3. Cut four 1½" by fabric width strips blue/green dot. Subcut into seven 15½" L pieces.

4. Cut four J strips, 1½" x 3½" from dark brown print.

5. Subcut two of the die-cut green paisley strips into two 2½" x 21½" O border strips.

Completing the House Block

1. Sew one brown floral C and one blue/green dot C together along long edge; press seam toward blue/green dot C (Figure 1). Repeat to make two C/C units.

Figure 1

2. To make the roof unit, sew the two C/C units together, matching the roof edges, again referring to Figure 1; press seam open.

3. Arrange and sew nine assorted B squares together in three rows of three squares each (Figure 2). Press seams in opposite directions in each row.

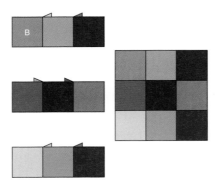

Figure 2

4. Sew the rows together to make one nine-patch house, again referring to Figure 2; press seams in one direction.

5. Sew one blue/green dot I strip to each side of the house to make a house unit (Figure 3); press seams toward I strips.

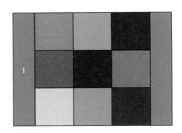

Figure 3

6. Sew the roof unit to the top of the house unit referring to the House block diagram; press seam toward house.

7. Repeat steps 1–6 to make a total of four House blocks.

Completing the Tree Block

1. Sew one blue/green dot E triangle to one side of a light green D triangle as shown in Figure 4; press seam toward E. Repeat with a second E triangle on the opposite side of the D triangle, again referring to Figure 4.

Figure 4

2. Repeat using one each of remaining three shades of green to make a total of four D/E units.

3. Sew one blue/green dot K strip to each long side of the J trunk strip (Figure 5); press seams toward J.

Figure 5

4. Referring to the Tree block diagram, arrange four D/E units and the J/K unit in a column with the lightest green D/E unit at the top and the darkest green D/E unit above the J/K unit. Sew the units together; press seams in one direction.

5. Repeat steps 1–4 to make four Tree blocks.

Completing the Bed Runner

1. Arrange and sew the Tree and House blocks with L sashing strips between each block, referring to Figure 6, to complete the runner center.

Figure 6

2. Sew two 2½" brown print strips together along short ends; press seam open. Cut one 79½" M strip.

3. Sew M to the bottom of the runner center, again referring to Figure 6.

4. Sew two of the fabric-width green paisley strips together along short ends; repeat. Press seams open. Cut two 79½" N border from each strip.

5. Sew the N borders to the top and bottom of the runner, referring to the Placement Diagram; press seams toward N.

6. Sew one O border strip to each side of the runner, again referring to the Placement Diagram; press seams toward O.

7. Layer and baste pieced top, batting and backing, referring to Finishing Your Quilt on page 6 of General Instructions.

8. Machine-quilt in the ditch of all seams.

9. Using the size 12 pearl cotton and a big stitch, hand-quilt ½" in from the tree edges, 1½" in from the roof

edges and diagonally through the nine-patch house unit as shown in Figure 7.

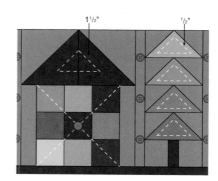

Figure 7

10. Sew a tan button to the center of each house nine-patch. Sew three green buttons down the center of each sashing strip, again referring to Figure 7.

11. To complete the quilt, bind using seven brown print 2½" strips, referring to Finishing Your Quilt on page 6 of General Instructions. ❖

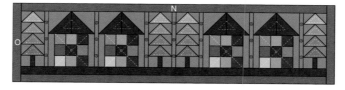

Row House Bed Runner
Placement Diagram 83" x 21"

Crossings

Design by Gina Gempesaw
Quilted by Carole Whaling

Make a bed-size quilt FAST! Feature large-scale prints in extra-large blocks.
A twist on the sashing treatment is a refreshing surprise.

Project Notes

The fabric colors and prints in this quilt are very similar to one another. Be careful to keep your fabrics and die-cut shapes organized. It may be helpful to cut a small swatch from each fabric and attach to a sheet of paper to create a fabric reference chart.

Refer to AccuQuilt GO!® die-cutting general instructions on page 3, for specific die-cutting processes.

Project Specifications

Skill Level: Advanced
Quilt Size: 90" x 90"
Block Size: 6" x 6"
Number of Blocks: 80

Materials

- ⅓ yard light blue
- ⅓ yard each of 3 different large-scale floral prints
- 1 yard coordinating stripe for binding
- 1¼ yards blue print
- 1⅞ yards dark green tonal
- 2 yards green print
- 2¼ yards green dot
- 2½ yards large floral stripe repeat for borders
- 3 yards brown print
- Backing 98" x 98"
- Batting 98" x 98"
- Neutral-color all-purpose thread
- AccuQuilt GO! fabric cutter
- AccuQuilt dies:
    GO! Mix & Match A (55000), B (55006), E (55009),
    G (55004) and H (55005)
- Basic quilting tools and supplies

AB
6" x 6" Block
Make 4

ABB
6" x 6" Block
Make 4

B1
6" x 6" Block
Make 28

B2
6" x 6" Block
Make 8

GE1
6" x 6" Block
Make 12

GE2
6" x 6" Block
Make 8

GE3
6" x 6" Block
Make 8

GE4
6" x 6" Block
Make 8

Die-Cutting Instructions

Note: Sort A, B, E and H shapes into color groups. Keep E and G shapes in mirror-image pairs as cut.

1. Cut two 7½" by fabric width strips green print and fan-fold 7½" wide. Die-cut eight A squares.

2. Cut four 7½" by fabric width strips blue print and fan-fold 7½" wide. Die-cut 16 A squares.

3. Cut two 7½" by fabric width strips dark green tonal and fan-fold 7½" wide. Die-cut 8 A squares.

4. Cut two 7½" by fabric width strips brown print and fan-fold 7½" wide. Die-cut eight A squares.

5. Cut five 8" by fabric width strips green dot and fan-fold 4½" wide. Die-cut 80 B squares.

6. Cut one 8" by fabric width strip light blue and fan-fold 4½" wide. Die-cut 16 B squares.

7. Cut four 8" by fabric width strips brown print and fan-fold 4½" wide. Die-cut 60 B squares.

8. Cut three 9½" by fabric width strips green dot and fan-fold 4½" wide. Die-cut 72 E triangles.

9. Cut one 9½" by fabric width strip green print and fan-fold 4½" wide. Die-cut 16 E triangles.

10. Cut one 9½" by fabric width strip blue print and fan-fold 4½" wide. Die-cut 32 E triangles.

11. Cut one 9½" by fabric width strip brown print and fan-fold 4½" wide. Die-cut 24 E triangles.

12. Cut (12) 3¾" by fabric width strips dark green tonal. Place strips right sides together in pairs. Die-cut 36 mirror-image pairs of G parallelograms.

13. Cut five 7½" by fabric width strips green print and fan-fold 4½" wide. Die-cut 36 H rectangles.

14. Cut two 7½" by fabric width strips brown print and fan-fold 4½" wide. Die-cut 12 H rectangles.

Additional Cutting Instructions

1. Cut four 6½" by fabric width strips brown print. Subcut into eight I rectangles, 6½" x 18½".

2. Fussy-cut (13) 6½" x 6½" A squares with a flower in the center of each from large-scale floral prints using a rotary cutter or the A die.

3. Cut four 6½" by 78½" strips along fabric length from large floral stripe repeat, centering flower stripe on the strip width.

4. Cut at least 375" of 2½"-wide bias strips from the coordinating stripe for binding.

Completing the Four-Patch Blocks

1. Sew a green dot B to a brown print B (Figure 1). Press seam toward brown print B. Repeat to make 56 B/B units.

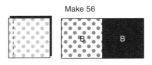

Make 56

Figure 1

2. Sew two B/B units together to make a Four-Patch block as shown in Figure 2. Press seams in one direction. Repeat to make 28 B1 blocks.

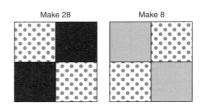

Make 28   Make 8

Figure 2

3. Repeat steps 1 and 2 using 16 each green dot B and light blue B to make eight B2 blocks (Figure 2).

Completing the Parallelogram Blocks

1. Choose a pair each of G, brown print E and green dot E. Referring to Figure 3, sew E triangles to G parallelograms to make two mirror-image units. Press seams on units in opposite directions.

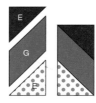

Figure 3

2. Match seams and sew mirror-image units together along long edge to make a chevron parallelogram block (Figure 4). Repeat to make 12 GE1 blocks.

Make 12

Figure 4

3. Referring to Figure 5 and with attention to color placement, choose a pair each of G and green dot E, and one each of green print E and blue print E shapes. Sew pieces together to make one unit with a blue print E top left corner and one unit with a green print E top right corner. Press seams on units in opposite directions.

Figure 5

4. Match seams and sew units together along long edge to make a chevron parallelogram block (Figure 5). Repeat to make eight GE2 blocks.

5. Referring to Figure 6 and with attention to color placement, choose a pair each of G and green dot E, and one each of green print E and blue print E shapes. Sew pieces together to make one unit with a green print E top left corner and one unit with a blue print E top right corner. Press seams on units in opposite directions.

Figure 6

6. Match seams and sew units together along long edge to make a chevron parallelogram block (Figure 6). Repeat to make eight GE3 blocks.

7. Choose a pair each of G, blue print E and green dot E. Referring to Figure 7, sew E triangles to G parallelograms to make two mirror-image units. Press seams on units in opposite directions.

Figure 7

8. Match seams and sew mirror-image units together along long edge to make a chevron parallelogram block (Figure 7). Repeat to make eight GE4 blocks.

Completing the Corner Blocks

1. Mark a diagonal line on the wrong side of four brown print B and eight green dot B.

2. Place one green dot B on the corner of a dark green tonal A. Sew on the marked diagonal. Trim seam to ¼". Press toward A (Figure 8). Make eight AB blocks. *Note: Four AB blocks will be used in the next step to create the ABB blocks.*

Figure 8

3. Place one brown print B on the corner opposite the green dot B of an AB block. Sew on the marked diagonal. Trim seam to ¼". Press toward A (Figure 9). Make four ABB blocks.

Figure 9

Completing the Units

1. Sew one ABB block and one brown print A square together as shown in Figure 10. Press seam toward A.

Figure 10

2. Sew a brown print A square to a B1 block as shown in Figure 10. Press seam toward A.

3. Sew ABB/A and A/B1 together to create Unit 1 as shown in Figure 10. Press seam in one direction. Repeat to make four of Unit 1.

4. Sew a green print A square between two B1 blocks, as shown in Figure 11. Press seams toward A.

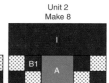

Figure 11

5. Sew a brown print I rectangle to the top of the A/B1 piece (Figure 11). Press seam toward I. Repeat to make eight of Unit 2.

House of White Birches, Berne, Indiana 46711   Clotilde.com

6. Sew a B2 block to the left side and a B1 block to the right side of a blue print A square as shown in Figure 12 to make the top row of Unit 3. Repeat to make four top rows.

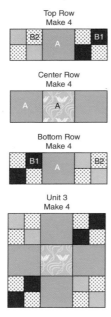

Top Row
Make 4

Center Row
Make 4

Bottom Row
Make 4

Unit 3
Make 4

Figure 12

7. Sew a large-scale floral print A between two blue print A squares to make the center row of Unit 3 (Figure 12). Repeat to make four center rows.

8. Sew a B1 block to the left side and a B2 block to the right side of a blue print A square to make the bottom row of Unit 3 (Figure 12). Repeat to make four bottom rows.

9. Sew top, center and bottom rows together to make four of Unit 3 as shown in Figure 12.

10. Sew a brown print H to the top of a GE1 block and a green print H to the bottom (Figure 13). Repeat to make 12 of Unit 4.

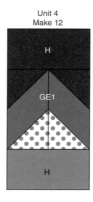

Unit 4
Make 12

Figure 13

11. Sew a GE2 and GE3 block together with green print and blue print E triangles matching (Figure 14). Sew green print H rectangles to both ends as shown in Figure 14. Repeat to make eight of Unit 5.

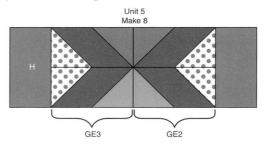

Unit 5
Make 8

GE3   GE2

Figure 14

12. Sew two GE4 blocks with blue print E triangles matching (Figure 15). Sew green print H rectangles to both ends as shown in Figure 15. Repeat to make four of Unit 6.

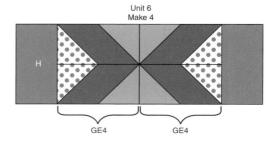

Unit 6
Make 4

GE4   GE4

Figure 15

Assembling the Quilt

Note: Throughout assembly, refer to Figure 16 for stitching order and orientation to make rows.

1. Sew two Unit 1, three Unit 4 and two Unit 2 together to make Row 1.

2. Sew two Unit 4, three large-scale floral A and two Unit 5 together to make Row 2.

3. Sew two Unit 2, two Unit 5, one Unit 6 and two Unit 3 together to make Row 3.

4. Sew two Unit 4, three large-scale floral A and two Unit 6 together to make Row 4.

5. Sew two Unit 2, two Unit 5, one Unit 6 and two Unit 3 together to make Row 5.

6. Sew two Unit 4, three large-scale floral A and two Unit 5 together to make Row 6.

7. Sew two Unit 1, three Unit 4 and two Unit 2 together to make Row 7.

8. Sew rows together in numerical order top to bottom, to complete the quilt center.

9. Sew two J border strips to opposite sides of quilt center.

10. Sew AB blocks to short ends of two J border strips and sew to quilt top and bottom referring to Placement Diagram for orientation.

11. Layer, quilt and bind, using the 2½" bias strips from coordinating stripe, following Finishing Your Quilt on page 6 of General Instructions. ❖

Tip

For shapes like Mix & Match G (parallelogram) and D (4⅞" triangle) that are not suggested to be fan-folded, open fabric strips out flat. Layer fabric strips, if desired, and cut one set and then continue to move strip over to cut across the width of the fabric.

—Gina Gempesaw

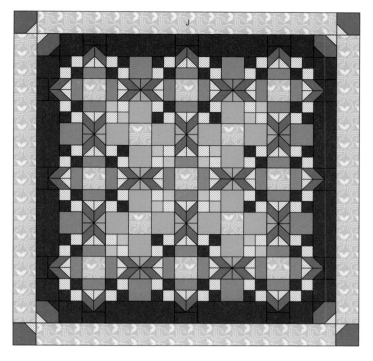

Crossings
Placement Diagram 90" x 90"

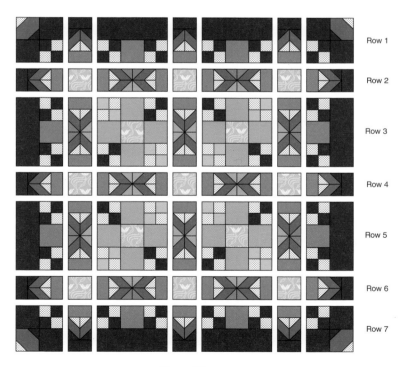

Row 1

Row 2

Row 3

Row 4

Row 5

Row 6

Row 7

Figure 16

GO! GO! GO!

Designed & Quilted by Gina Gempesaw

A playful little quilt for your favorite tyke features
wood-block cars and the word "GO" in the borders.

Project Note

Refer to AccuQuilt GO!® die-cutting general instructions
on page 3, for specific die-cutting processes.

Project Specifications

Skill Level: Intermediate
Quilt Size: 52" x 52"
Block Size: 12" x 12", 12" x 12", and 12" x 11"
Number of Blocks: 8, 4 and 4

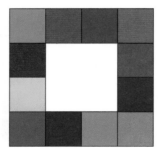

G
12" x 12" Block
Make 4

O
12" x 12" Block
Make 4

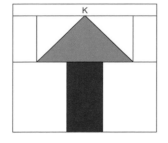

Arrow
12" x 11" Block
Make 4

Materials

- 14 fat quarters of assorted bright prints and solids
- ⅝ yard bright print

- 2⅓ yards white
- ¼ yard paper-backed fusible web
- Backing 60" x 60"
- Batting 60" x 60"
- All-purpose thread to match fabrics
- Clear monofilament thread
- AccuQuilt GO! fabric cutter
- AccuQuilt dies:
    GO! Mix & Match A (55000), B (55006), C (55001),
    D (55002) and H (55005)
    GO! Strip Cutter—2½" (55017)
    GO! Circle—2", 3" and 5" (55012)
- Basic quilting tools and supplies

Die-Cutting Instructions

1. Cut one 8" x 22" strip from each fat quarter and fan-fold 4½" wide. Die-cut each strip into eight B squares to make at least 101 B squares.

2. Die-cut four C triangles from a variety of fat quarters.

3. Die-cut 13 H rectangles from a variety of fat quarters.

4. Cut three 7½" x fabric width strips white and fan-fold two strips 7½" wide. Die-cut eight A squares. Fan-fold one strip 4½" wide and die-cut six H rectangles.

5. Cut one 8" x fabric width strip white and die-cut into 10 B squares.

6. Cut one 4½" x fabric width strip white and die-cut eight D triangles.

7. Cut two 8½" x fabric width strips white and one 3½" x fabric width strip white. Die-cut into seven 2½" x fabric strips using the 2½" strip cutter. Cut 2½" strips into two O borders 28½" long, two M sashing strips 24½" long, six 12½" P strips and eight 4½" x 2½" J rectangles.

8. Cut two 8½" x fabric width strips from bright print yardage. Die-cut six 2½" x fabric width strips using the 2½" strip cutter for binding.

Additional Cutting Instructions

1. Cut two 3½" x fabric width strips white. Subcut into two 24½" N strips and six 3½" x 2" L rectangles.

2. Cut four 1½" x fabric width strips white. Subcut into (12) 12½" K strips.

3. Cut one 6½" x fabric width strip white. Subcut into eight 6½" x 5" I rectangles.

Preparing Appliqué

1. Choose a variety of nine pairs of bright scraps at least 3½" x 3½". Apply paper-backed fusible web to back of scraps following manufacturer's instructions.

2. Using the circle die set or templates provided, individually cut nine pairs of 2" circles. Set circle pairs aside.

Completing G & O Blocks

1. Choose a variety of 44 bright B squares and four white B squares. Referring to Figure 1, sew 32 of the bright B squares into eight sets of four squares. Sew eight of the bright B squares into four sets of two squares (Figure 1). Press seams in one direction. Sew a white B square to each of the remaining four bright B squares to make four sets (Figure 1). Press seams in one direction.

Figure 1

2. Sew a set of two bright B squares to the left side of A (Figure 2). Press seams toward A. Sew a bright B and white B set to the right side of A (Figure 2). Press seams toward A.

Figure 2

3. Sew a set of four bright B squares to top and bottom of A/B unit to make a G block, referring to Figure 3. Press seams toward A. Repeat steps 2 and 3 to make four G blocks.

Figure 3

4. Choose a variety of 48 bright B squares. Sew 32 of the squares into eight sets of four B squares and 16 of the squares into eight sets of two B squares (Figure 4). Press seams in one direction.

Figure 4

5. Sew a set of two B squares to the right and left side of A, press seams toward A. Sew a set of four B squares to top and bottom of A/B unit to make an O block (Figure 5). Press seams toward A.

Figure 5

6. Repeat step 5 to make four O blocks.

Completing Arrow Blocks

1. Sew D triangles to either side of a C triangle to make a C/D rectangle (Figure 6). Press seams toward D. Sew a J rectangle to both short ends of C/D; press seams toward J to make a Z row (Figure 6). Repeat to make four Z rows.

Figure 6

2. Sew an I rectangle on both long sides of a bright print H (Figure 7). Press seams toward H to make a Y row. Repeat to make four Y rows.

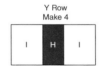

Figure 7

3. Referring to the Arrow block diagram, sew a Z row to top of a Y row. Press seams toward Y row. Sew K strip to top of Z row; press seam toward K. Repeat to make four Arrow blocks.

Completing Car Rows

1. Choose three bright B squares and two each white H and L rectangles. Referring to Figure 8 for placement, sew squares and rectangles together. Repeat to make three L/B/H rows.

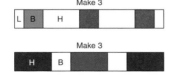

Figure 8

2. Choose two white B squares and three bright H rectangles. Referring to Figure 8 for placement, sew squares and rectangles together. Repeat to make three H/B rows.

3. Sew an L/B/H row to an H/B row. Repeat to make three car rows.

Completing the Quilt

1. Sew M sashing strips between car rows and N strips to top and bottom of car rows (Figure 9). Sew O strips to both sides of car rows unit to complete quilt center (Figure 9).

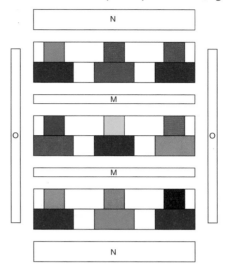

Figure 9

2. For each car, choose a pair of 2" circles, remove paper backing. Fuse circles to car bodies, overlapping bright H rectangles, and M and lower N strips for car wheels, referring to Placement Diagram for positioning.

3. Using a buttonhole stitch, sew around each wheel with coordinating or clear monofilament thread.

4. Sew a K strip to the H/I edge of two Arrow blocks and a P strip to the H/I edge of remaining two Arrow blocks (Figure 10). Press seams toward K or P strips.

Figure 10

5. To make top border, sew one each K/Arrow block (pointing up), K, G block, P, O block and P/Arrow block (pointing right) together referring to Figure 11 for placement and orientation. Press seams toward K and P strips.

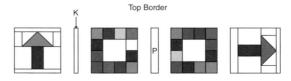

Figure 11

6. To make bottom border, sew one each P/Arrow block (pointing left), G block, P, O block, K, and K/Arrow block (pointing down) together referring to Figure 12 for placement and orientation. Press seams toward K and P strips.

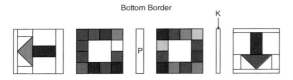

Figure 12

7. Referring to Figure 13, sew a K strip to left side of a G block. Sew P between the K/G block and an O block. Sew a K strip to the right side of the O block. Press seams toward K and P. Repeat to make two GO side units.

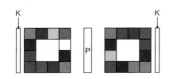

Figure 13

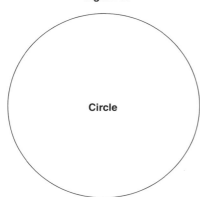

Circle

8. Referring to the Placement Diagram for positioning, sew a GO side unit to each side of the quilt center to make center row. Sew top border to top of center row and bottom border to bottom of center row to complete quilt top. Press seams toward quilt center.

9. Layer, quilt and bind, using 2½" bright print strips, following Finishing Your Quilt on page 6 of General Instructions. ❖

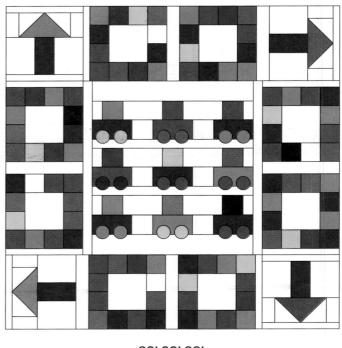

GO! GO! GO!
Placement Diagram 52" x 52"

Special Thanks & Supplies

Thank you to AccuQuilt for providing GO!® Fabric Cutters and dies to our talented team of designers.

Page 8: Stepping Stones—Arnold's Attic fabric by Barbara Brackman for Moda.

Page 12: Waterfall—Batiks provided by Moda.

Page 21: Bursting Into Bloom—Yippee … Daisies! Fabric Collection and Tokyo Basics from Red Rooster Fabrics, Steam-A-Seam2® from the Warm Company, Blendables® thread from Sulky®.

Page 26: Flash of Lightning—Frolic by Sandy Gervais for Moda, Thermore® batting by Hobbs Bonded Fibers.

Page 30: Garden Trellis—Martinique and Aster Manor fabrics by 3 Sisters for Moda, Thermore® batting by Hobbs Bonded Fibers.

Page 35: Points of Interest—Blendables® thread from Sulky®.

Page 40: Imperial Gardens Place Mats—Imperial Fusions Collection: Kyoto from Robert Kaufman.

Page 51: Crossings—Coquette by Carina Gardner for Northcott Fabrics.

Page 58: GO! GO! GO!—Oodles of Doodles and Rhapsodie Colorée II by Ricky Tims for Red Rooster, Naturally Naturals II from Red Rooster.

Photo Index

8

12

16

21

26

30

35

40

43

47

51

58

House of White Birches, Berne, Indiana 46711   Clotilde.com

Metric Conversion Charts

Metric Conversions

Canada/U.S. Measurement		Multiplied by		Metric Measurement
yards	x	.9144	=	metres (m)
yards	x	91.44	=	centimetres (cm)
inches	x	2.54	=	centimetres (cm)
inches	x	25.40	=	millimetres (mm)
inches	x	.0254	=	metres (m)

Canada/U.S. Measurement		Multiplied by		Metric Measurement
centimetres	x	.3937	=	inches
metres	x	1.0936	=	yards

Standard Equivalents

Canada/U.S. Measurement				Metric Measurement
⅛ inch	=	3.20 mm	=	0.32 cm
¼ inch	=	6.35 mm	=	0.635 cm
⅜ inch	=	9.50 mm	=	0.95 cm
½ inch	=	12.70 mm	=	1.27 cm
⅝ inch	=	15.90 mm	=	1.59 cm
¾ inch	=	19.10 mm	=	1.91 cm
⅞ inch	=	22.20 mm	=	2.22 cm
1 inch	=	25.40 mm	=	2.54 cm
⅛ yard	=	11.43 cm	=	0.11 m
¼ yard	=	22.86 cm	=	0.23 m
⅜ yard	=	34.29 cm	=	0.34 m
½ yard	=	45.72 cm	=	0.46 m
⅝ yard	=	57.15 cm	=	0.57 m
¾ yard	=	68.58 cm	=	0.69 m
⅞ yard	=	80.00 cm	=	0.80 m
1 yard	=	91.44 cm	=	0.91 m
1⅛ yards	=	102.87 cm	=	1.03 m
1¼ yards	=	114.30 cm	=	1.14 m

Canada/U.S. Measurement		Metric Measurement		Metric Measurement
1⅜ yards	=	125.73 cm	=	1.26 m
1½ yards	=	137.16 cm	=	1.37 m
1⅝ yards	=	148.59 cm	=	1.49 m
1¾ yards	=	160.02 cm	=	1.60 m
1⅞ yards	=	171.44 cm	=	1.71 m
2 yards	=	182.88 cm	=	1.83 m
2⅛ yards	=	194.31 cm	=	1.94 m
2¼ yards	=	205.74 cm	=	2.06 m
2⅜ yards	=	217.17 cm	=	2.17 m
2½ yards	=	228.60 cm	=	2.29 m
2⅝ yards	=	240.03 cm	=	2.40 m
2¾ yards	=	251.46 cm	=	2.51 m
2⅞ yards	=	262.88 cm	=	2.63 m
3 yards	=	274.32 cm	=	2.74 m
3⅛ yards	=	285.75 cm	=	2.86 m
3¼ yards	=	297.18 cm	=	2.97 m
3⅜ yards	=	308.61 cm	=	3.09 m
3½ yards	=	320.04 cm	=	3.20 m
3⅝ yards	=	331.47 cm	=	3.31 m
3¾ yards	=	342.90 cm	=	3.43 m
3⅞ yards	=	354.32 cm	=	3.54 m
4 yards	=	365.76 cm	=	3.66 m
4⅛ yards	=	377.19 cm	=	3.77 m
4¼ yards	=	388.62 cm	=	3.89 m
4⅜ yards	=	400.05 cm	=	4.00 m
4½ yards	=	411.48 cm	=	4.11 m
4⅝ yards	=	422.91 cm	=	4.23 m
4¾ yards	=	434.34 cm	=	4.34 m
4⅞ yards	=	445.76 cm	=	4.46 m
5 yards	=	457.20 cm	=	4.57 m

HOUSE of WHITE BIRCHES PUBLISHERS SINCE 1947

Mix & Match Quilts With the AccuQuilt GO! is published by DRG, 306 East Parr Road, Berne, IN 46711. Printed in USA. Copyright © 2010 DRG. All rights reserved. This publication may not be reproduced in part or in whole without written permission from the publisher.

RETAIL STORES: If you would like to carry this pattern book or any other DRG publications, visit DRGwholesale.com

Every effort has been made to ensure that the instructions in this pattern book are complete and accurate. We cannot, however, take responsibility for human error, typographical mistakes or variations in individual work. Please visit ClotildeCustomerCare.com to check for pattern updates.

ISBN: 978-1-59217-332-7

1 2 3 4 5 6 7 8 9